Weird

But

True

200 Astounding, Outrageous, and Totally Off the Wall Facts

Leslie Gilbert Elman

FALL RIVER PRESS

Book design by James Sarfati

Fall River Press
122 Fifth Avenue
New York, NY 10011

ISBN: 978-1-4351-2678-7

Printed and bound in the United States of America

10 9 8 7 6

"Truth is stranger than Fiction, but it is because Fiction is obliged to stick to possibilities, Truth isn't."

—Mark Twain

Introduction

*a*ll the wild fantasies dreamed up by novelists, artists, and filmmakers, often don't compare to the oddball discoveries made every year by researchers around the world. Nobody would believe a novel that included a suicidal tree—but you can see one for yourself in Madagascar. A film that featured a floating raft of garbage the size of Texas would seem fantastic—scientists say there's one in the Pacific Ocean that's *at least* that large.

If you're fascinated by the strange, unusual, and unexplainable truths of our world (and who isn't?), just turn the page...

The Facts
as We Know
Them...

You Wash, I'll Dry

*T*here are 16 million thunderstorms on Earth every year. In January 2010 a man in Sydney, Australia, was struck by lightning while he was doing the dishes at the kitchen sink. During the same storm, lightning entered another home through an open window and set the curtains on fire.

1

Don't Answer That

*T*he most common victims of indoor lightning strikes are people who are talking on the phone during a storm. Landline telephones conduct electricity.

WEIRD BUT TRUE

What's the Frequency, Earth?

*E*arth broadcasts a symphony of sound—crackles, pops, whistles, and sizzles—via radio waves that result from lightning strikes. No lightning in your area? No problem. Even storms on the other side of the planet can send these very low frequency (VLF) radio waves bouncing between the surface of the planet and the ionosphere—boing, boing, boing—all the way to your house. Typical radio receivers won't detect them, but special VLF receivers will.

3

Fueling Fossils

*W*hen lightning strikes a place where the soil is sandy, its heat causes the silica in the sand to form craggy glass tubes that "fossilize" the lightning. Fossilized lightning bolts are called "fulgurites."

* * *

Fulgur is the Latin word for "lightning."

Lightning in the Desert

a fulgurite estimated to be about fifteen thousand years old was found in the Sahara. Because a rainstorm almost always accompanies lightning, geochronologists (scientists who specialize in determining the age of rocks) believe this fulgurite is evidence that the Sahara was not always the hot, dry environment we know today.

The 2,000-Year-Old Poop

To make a case for linking the Dead Sea Scrolls to the strict religious sect called the Essenes, scholars did a little digging in the . . . er . . . dirt near where the scrolls were discovered. There they found a 2,000-year-old communal latrine where the Essenes did their business and, following the laws of the Bible word for word, buried their poop. The poop itself was long gone, but they found traces of human intestinal parasites such as tapeworms that had been buried in the soil for thousands of years.

More Poop

*a*rchaeologists working at Paisley Caves in Oregon in 2002 found human poop that they have determined to be 14,300 years old—the oldest traces of human life ever found in North America.

* * *

Polite archaeologists call fossilized poop "coprolites."

7

Dig It

$\mathcal{I}$n England during the nineteenth century, coprolite mining became an important industry. The fossilized dinosaur dung (for that's what it was!) was loaded with phosphates used to make the first artificial fertilizer for agricultural crops.

* * *

There's a Coprolite Street in Ipswich, England.

8

Island Time

*M*adagascar, the island nation off the east coast of Africa, is a favorite spot for paleontologists in search of dinosaur bones. Among their finds have been the remains of a mini 2.5-foot crocodile that lived on land, a cannibalistic dinosaur, and a creature that researchers call *Masiakasaurus knopfleri*. This last dinosaur was named for the lead singer/guitarist of the band Dire Straits because the crew realized that every time Dire Straits music was played at the dig site they found another dinosaur bone.

9

Late Bloomer

*M*ore than 170 species of palm trees live on Madagascar, but as far as botanists know, only one is suicidal. The species, called *Tahina spectabilis*, can grow to more than sixty feet tall with leaves sixteen feet in diameter. A tree that big is hard to miss, but it took until 2007 for botanists to realize that unlike most palms, which flower regularly throughout their lives, this one produces flowers only once—and then collapses to the ground and dies. "[It] flowers itself to death," said a member of the multinational team that published a scientific paper on the new species. "It's an amazing way to go."

WEIRD BUT TRUE

Stinko Ginkgo

Ginkgo trees come in male and female varieties. Female trees produce fruit that contains butyric acid, which smells (depending on whom you ask) like rancid butter or vomit.

* * *

About one in every two hundred male ginkgo trees also will produce these putrid fruits.

11

Still Standing

a handful of ginkgo trees survived the atomic bomb assault on the Japanese city of Hiroshima during World War II. They are still alive today.

12

Color My World

*a*utumn leaves in Europe tend to be mostly yellow, while those in North America turn orange and red as well. The seasonal change in color depends upon what happens to the chlorophyll in the leaves. Leaves turn yellow when the green chlorophyll in them breaks down, allowing the leaves' natural yellow pigment to show through. Leaves turn red because they start to produce a new red pigment (called "anthocyanin," if you're keeping track) when the chlorophyll breaks down. Why the latter occurs in North America and not in Europe is still a subject for debate and research.

Red, Red Dye

*T*he natural coloring used to make foods, cosmetics, and such toiletries as shampoo red or orange comes from the crushed bodies of female cochineal beetles found in Peru, Mexico, and the Canary Islands. It takes about seventy thousand insects to yield one pound of dye.

Whiter Than White

𝓑ecause pure white bread was considered to be of higher quality than brown bread, medieval bakers would whiten their flour by any means necessary—mixing it with alum, chalk, clay, or even ground bones.

Shame, Shame!

*I*n fourteenth-century England and France, bakers who were caught tampering with the purity of their bread were punished by being led through the streets and to the pillory with a loaf of bread tied around their neck. If they were caught a second time, they might be beaten or their ovens destroyed. After a third offense, they would be run out of town.

WEIRD BUT TRUE

It All Went Sour

*I*n medieval times, a German tavern owner and his wife who had tried to sweeten sour wine by mixing it with roasted pears were punished by being locked in the pillory with pears hung around their necks.

The Price of Spice

*O*rdinary black pepper wasn't so ordinary way back when. In fact, it used to be so rare and valuable that when the Visigoths sacked Rome in the fifth century they demanded three thousand pounds of pepper (among other riches) as ransom for the city's release.

* * *

Pepper was sometimes included in dowries during the Middle Ages.

Put Some Pepper on It

*W*hat do you call a single woman who's over thirty? In Scandinavia, she's a "pepper maiden" (*pebermø* in Danish; *piparmey* in Icelandic). A single guy over thirty is a "pepper man" (*pebersvend* in Danish; *piparsveinn* in Icelandic). The terms hark back to the fourteenth-century German merchants who worked in Scandinavia but were not allowed to marry there. Those salesmen and traders—many of whom sold spices, including pepper— were the only older single guys around. Today it's common for people in Denmark, Norway, and Iceland to celebrate a single friend's thirtieth birthday by presenting him or her with peppermills as gag gifts.

19

WEIRD BUT TRUE

I Do

*I*n the United States, the probability of a woman being married by age thirty is 74 percent; for a man it's 61 percent.

Boys and Girls Together

*S*ome giant Australian cuttlefish are more "giant" than others, and when it comes to wooing the alluring female giant Australian cuttlefish, the smaller males are no match for their beefier brethren. So instead of going head to head with the big boys, the smaller guys hang out with the gals—even changing color to resemble the females. Then they sneak up on the females and mate with them on the sly.

* * *

The nematode worm goes even further than that. It actually changes sex to increase its chances of mating. And if a female can't find a mate, that's no problem at all—she has the ability to self-fertilize and produce her own offspring, all of which are born female.

21

We're All Ladies Here

*T*he speckled insects of the family *Coccinellidae* are known as ladybugs in the United States, and as ladybirds in England, Australia, India, and Pakistan. Entomologists prefer to call them lady beetles, but they have many other names as well, including lady cows and lady flies. The Russian word for ladybug translates to "God's little cow." In Turkish it's "good luck beetle," and in Hebrew it's "Moses's cow."

* * *

All ladybugs are referred to as ladybugs—even if they're male.

22

Sharks are Doin' It For Themselves

*T*idbit, a female blacktip shark, grew up in an aquarium in Virginia and had no contact with male blacktip sharks for the eight years of her life. So imagine how surprised her handlers were when she turned up pregnant. Tidbit's pregnancy confirmed what ichthyologists (fish biologists) had long suspected: Sharks have the ability to reproduce by virgin birth. Female sharks can become pregnant without the assistance of males, and those offspring have the same DNA as their moms without any contributions from another shark. Ichthyologists believe that this type of reproduction could become even more common as shark populations are overfished and females have a tougher time finding mates.

23

Love Bites

The skin of female blue sharks and Greenland sharks is twice as thick as that of their male counterparts. That's because sharks mate face-to-face, and the males of these species bite the females violently to hold them in place while copulating.

24

That's Harsh

$\mathcal{M}$ ost sharks live in tropical or temperate waters, but the Greenland shark likes it cold—really cold. It's found as far north as the Arctic, and it spends much of its time in the deepest, darkest parts of the ocean.

Dark and Deep

*P*arasites attach themselves to the Greenland shark's eyes, damaging the corneas and leaving the shark virtually blind. Since its habitat is pitch-dark anyway, this isn't as detrimental as it might sound. The Greenland shark uses its other senses to detect prey, and it's not a picky eater—it will consume anything that crosses its path.

* * *

The stomach contents of one Greenland shark included seals, squid, fish, nematode worms, rope, fishing nets, and pieces of wood.

26

WEIRD BUT TRUE

Life as We Are Getting to Know It

*T*here are some pretty bizarre life-forms in the world, and many of them live in incredibly harsh surroundings. Take the microbes that thrive in the purely acidic, sulfur-ridden environments of hot springs in Japan—environments that would literally strip the skin from your bones if given the chance. These little buggers are called *Picrophilus torridus* (*Picrophilus* means "acid-loving;" *torridus* means "hot"), and they live in extremely hot conditions with a pH of near zero. Thermoacidophiles like these are the type of organism scientists point to when they wonder about life-forms that might exist on other planets. Would the acid environments of Mars or Venus keep them away? Probably not. In fact, these microbes might be out there in the galaxy soaking up the sulfur right now. . . .

27

Trial
Blazing

*S*cientists working at the U.S. Department of Energy's Brookhaven National Laboratory recently created the highest temperature ever recorded in the universe: 7.2 trillion degrees Fahrenheit. That's 250,000 times hotter than the core of the sun.

In an Absolute World

*W*hen something is heated, the molecules within it move faster. When something is cooled, the molecules within it move slower. How can you make the molecules stop entirely? Bring them to absolute zero on the Kelvin temperature scale (about –459°F or –273°C). But that's easier said than done. Physicists haven't been able to create an absolute zero temperature yet (it can exist only under controlled conditions). They've missed it by about a billionth of a degree.

29

Absolute Hotness

*W*hile there is an accepted concept of absolute zero among scientists with regard to temperature, there is no universally accepted concept of absolute hotness.

To a Degree

*O*n the Celsius or centigrade scale, 0° is the temperature at which water freezes and 100° is water's boiling point. But that's not how Anders Celsius intended it to be. When the Swedish astronomer introduced his temperature scale in 1742, he placed the boiling point at 0° and the freezing point at 100°

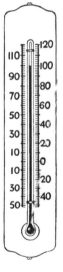

Hot Topic

*S*wedish botanist Carolus Linnaeus was probably the one who turned the Celsius thermometer upside down. Linnaeus is best known for devising the Latin binomial nomenclature we humans (or, as Linnaeus would say, *Homo sapiens*) still use to describe plants, animals, and minerals today.

* * *

Linnaeus unveiled his change to the Celsius thermometer in December 1745, about a year after Celsius's death.

Cold Comfort

$\mathcal{F}$rederic Tudor of Boston made his fortune by harvesting ice from the frozen ponds of Massachusetts and transporting it to places that didn't have ice of their own. His first international delivery was to the Caribbean island of Martinique in 1806. By 1833 he was shipping ice from New England to India.

* * *

The first ship delivering ice to India left Boston with 180 tons of ice and arrived with 100 tons—the rest had melted on the journey.

33

WEIRD BUT TRUE

Not as Clear as You'd Think

*W*ater rarely freezes at precisely 0°C, and sometimes hot water will freeze faster than cold water.

* * *

Hot water freezing faster than cold water is known as the Mpemba effect. It was named for a student in Tanzania, who during the 1960s, pointed out the phenomenon to his science teacher and asked for an explanation. Physicists are still searching for one.

Listen When Wet

*S*ound travels about three times faster through water than through air, and moves faster through salt water than fresh water.

Brr... Sounds Cold

*K*nowing the speed at which sound travels helps scientists measure the temperature of the ocean. Because temperature affects how fast sound travels through water, by timing how long it takes a sound to travel underwater from point A to point B, it's possible to gauge the temperature of the water around it. This process is called acoustic thermometry.

WEIRD BUT TRUE

Have You Ever Heard the Rain?

$\mathcal{I}$f you happen to be scuba diving during a rainstorm (definitely *not* a good idea!), the sound of the raindrops on the ocean's surface could drive you mad. Small raindrops produce a surprisingly loud sound when they hit the surface of the water—first a "plink," followed by a sharp ping like the ringing of a high-pitched bell. Large raindrops create more of a "plunk" sound, followed by a softer ping.

37

Raindrops Keep Fallin'

*P*hysicists have devised underwater recording devices that can measure the amount of rainfall over the open ocean by monitoring the sounds the rain makes when it hits the surface of the water.

WEIRD BUT TRUE

The Sound We All Hate

𝓕ingernails scraping a chalkboard. Just the mention of it probably makes you cringe, but you've probably never stopped to wonder why. Now you'll know: This action produces sound frequencies similar to those of a chimpanzee's warning call. So the sense of distress we feel when the fingernails scrape could be a sign that our fundamental primate danger sensors have been triggered.

39

The Ultimate Playlist

a 2009 study at the University of Wisconsin set out to determine how tamarin monkeys respond to various types of musical sounds. Classical? Jazz? Polka? Most human music left the monkeys cold—or even made them anxious—with one exception: They seemed to like the heavy metal sound of the band Metallica. The other tunes that turned them on were specially composed pieces that combined cello music with monkey calls.

Dance Party

Chimpanzees in Senegal have an unusual response to the wildfires that affect the grasslands where they live: The flames make them want to dance. Rather than running away or exhibiting other behaviors associated with fear, the chimps observe the fire, dance around it, and remain alert enough to avoid being burned when the fire spreads over the savanna.

41

WEIRD BUT TRUE

Right-Hand Turn

*C*himps gesture with their hands when they talk to each other, even going so far as to reach out their right hand to greet each other with what could be called a handshake.

42

Which Side Are You On?

*S*amoa changed its motor vehicle laws in 2009 to mandate that cars be driven on the left side of the road instead of the right. At the time, there were fewer than twenty thousand cars registered in Samoa.

* * *

Prior to the change in Samoa, the last nation to switch driving sides was Gnana, which switched from left to right in 1974.

43

Leaning Left

*a*bout one-third of the world's population lives in countries where cars are driven on the left side of the road. Among the nations that drive on the left are Australia, Botswana, India, Indonesia, Japan, Kenya, New Zealand, South Africa, Thailand, and the United Kingdom.

* * *

The U.S. Virgin Islands is the only U.S. territory in which people drive on the left.

Stay in Your Own Lane

In February 2009, the American Iridium 33 communications satellite collided with the inactive Russian Cosmos 2251 satellite over Siberia, about 491 miles above Earth. It's the first time such a collision has happened, but scientists fear it probably won't be the last. As of October 2009, there were approximately nine hundred working manmade satellites orbiting Earth and many other defunct satellites still floating around in space; it's possible that some of them will unintentionally end up colliding with each other.

45

That One's Ours

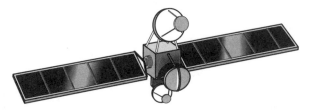

*a*lmost half of the working satellites in orbit today are from the United States.

* * *

The United States operates more than four times as many satellites as any other nation. Russia is second.

WEIRD BUT TRUE

Clean Up Your Junk

*O*rbital debris—better known as "space junk"—is a serious hazard. Think of what a random pebble kicked up on the highway can do to your car. Now, imagine billions of pieces of metallic garbage—everything from entire satellites to fuel tanks, nuts and bolts, and even tiny paint chips—zooming around in orbit at speeds of more than fifteen thousand miles per hour.

Now Look What You've Done!

$\mathcal{T}$he Iridium-Cosmos collision produced more than seven hundred new pieces of space junk. At present there are more than nineteen thousand pieces of space junk being tracked by authorities such as the U.S. Department of Defense.

Bang! Zoom!

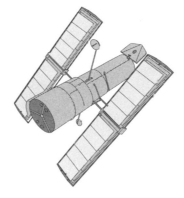

*B*etween 1994 and 2002, the solar panels on the Hubble Space Telescope were struck an estimated 725,000 times by space junk.

That's Ours, Too

*I*n 2010, the California State Historical Resources Commission designated the items left by Apollo 11 astronauts on the moon to be a state historical resource. This action could mark the first time that such a designation was given to something not on Earth.

* * *

The move was considered to be the first step toward having Tranquility Base (where the U.S. astronauts landed on the moon in 1969) declared a UNESCO World Heritage Site.

50

For Future Generations

*T*he list of more than one hundred items left on the moon by the Apollo 11 astronauts includes two pairs of space boots, tools, cameras, pieces of the Lunar Module spacecraft, airsickness bags, and containers used to collect the astronauts' urine and feces.

WEIRD BUT TRUE

Another Fine Mess

*T*here's a giant garbage patch floating in the Pacific Ocean between California and Hawaii. The part of it known as the Eastern Pacific Garbage Patch is roughly twice the size of the state of Texas. It is made up largely of plastic trash—soda bottles and the like—some of which has been carried on the currents from as far away as China.

* * *

By some estimates, the entire Great Pacific Garbage Patch stretches from California to Japan.

52

And Yet Another...

*I*n 2010 a similar garbage patch was discovered in the Atlantic Ocean spanning the distance between Virginia and Cuba.

WEIRD BUT TRUE

Ooh! That Smell

*C*an a clean-smelling room make you a better human being? Apparently so. A recent study at Brigham Young University found that people who live and work in clean-smelling environments treat others more fairly and act more charitably than those in rooms with no particular smell at all. To test the theory, researchers compared the behavior of people in rooms cleaned with citrus-scented spray cleaner with those in "unscented" rooms. The individuals in the citrus-scented group proved to be more trustworthy and more eager to volunteer their time and money for charitable causes.

Scent of a Crime

*J*ust as they have fingerprints, humans have "odor prints," and no two are the same. That's how bloodhounds can tell the difference between one person and another—even identical twins. This is great news for law enforcement: Even if a criminal doesn't leave fingerprints at the scene of a crime, his scent is still evident. By swabbing the scene, investigators can pick up identification traces that they can match with scent samples taken from suspects.

55

Sniffing Out the Enemy

*T*he former East German secret police—the Stasi—used specially designed seat cushions to collect odor samples from suspected enemies of the state during interrogations.

Uncommon Senses

*P*eople with synesthesia interpret sensory information in unusual ways. They might see letters and numbers in distinct colors, even if the printed type they're reading is black. They might taste sounds or hear colors—perceiving two separate sensory triggers where most people would perceive only one.

* * *

The number of people with some form of synesthesia has not been determined. It could be as high as one in every twenty people.

57

In the Mood for Love

*M*any male animals use their sense of smell when searching for a mate, and it turns out that this includes human males. A Florida State University study found that men's testosterone levels increased when they sniffed a T-shirt that had been worn by a woman who was ovulating.

One Last Kiss

*O*n a roadside in Grünstadt, Germany, a young man flagged down a passing car. When a female driver stopped to help him, he unfolded a map and asked her for directions. Distracted by the map, she didn't notice when he reached into the car and swiped her wallet. After she pointed out the route he was looking for, in a gentlemanly gesture, he kissed her hand and thanked her. When she discovered her wallet had been lifted, she went to the police, who swabbed the back of her hand and collected enough DNA evidence to identify the crook.

59

WEIRD BUT TRUE

No Spit!

*T*he protein composition of a woman's saliva changes as she ages.

60

Lullaby...

*C*hanges in hormone levels make it harder for a woman to sing when she's pregnant. Rising hormones affect the vocal folds so more lung pressure is needed to hit certain notes.

...And Good Night

*P*ossibly the world's most famous lullaby, the song that begins "Lullaby, and good night" was written by Johannes Brahms, who never married and had no children.

Sleep Tight

*N*S-RED stands for Nocturnal Sleep-Related Eating Disorder, also known as "sleep eating." Not only do sufferers leave their beds and wander around in their sleep, they make their way to the fridge and chow down—then remember nothing the morning after!

* * *

NS-RED affects twice as many women as men.

Don't Let the Bedbugs Bite!

*B*esides burrowing into mattresses, pillows, carpeting, and upholstered furniture, bedbugs can live in wood furniture, behind electrical outlets, under wallpaper, and inside picture frames, clocks, electronics, and smoke detectors.

* * *

When they feed, bedbugs can consume six times their body weight in human blood.

64

WEIRD BUT TRUE

Bugging Out

*J*ames Harrington, a political philosopher and friend of England's King Charles I, was imprisoned in the Tower of London in 1660. During his incarceration he came to believe that his perspiration turned into flies and bees.

Name It and Claim It

*K*arl-Axel Ekbom, a Swedish neurologist, published a detailed documentation of "delusional parasitosis" in 1938. His work was so significant that the disorder came to be known as Ekbom's Syndrome.

* * *

Ekbom also coined the term "restless legs syndrome" to describe the sensation of itching or creeping under the skin that compels a person to move her legs. RLS is sometimes referred to as Wittmaack-Ekbom Syndrome, named in part for German physician Theodor Wittmaack, who studied the disease in the 1850s.

Creepy Crawlies

*P*eople with the psychological disorder Ekbom's Syndrome believe they're infested with parasites crawling on and under their skin. The sensation is so real that they can both feel and see the imaginary bugs.

There's a Word for It

*E*kbom's Syndrome, or delusional parasitosis, is also known as formication. (Read that word carefully!)

* * *

Formica is the Latin word for "ant."

A Dollar
and a Dream

The building and surfacing material Formica was originally developed as insulation material for electrical devices. At the time, insulation was made mainly from the mineral mica. The new material was a substitute "for mica"—and that's how it got its name.

* * *

Daniel J. O'Conor and Herbert A. Faber were the Westinghouse engineers who developed Formica. When they filed their patent in 1913, the company paid them one dollar for the rights to their invention. They quit and set up their own business soon after.

69

Family Business

*W*illiam Procter, a candle maker, and James Gamble, a soap maker, went into business together because their father-in-law, Alexander Norris, suggested it. In 1837 they created the company known as Procter & Gamble.

99 and 44/100 Percent Pure

*P*rocter & Gamble's first major product was Ivory Soap, invented in 1879 by Gamble's son, James N. Gamble. It was named by Procter's son, Harley T. Procter, inspired by a passage from the Bible: Psalms 45:8, which refers to "ivory palaces."

71

It Floats

*I*vory Soap floats because there's air whipped into the mixture. This makes the soap lighter than water (and easy to find in the tub!).

WEIRD BUT TRUE

That Was Quick

*Y*ou'll always remain afloat in quicksand because the human body is less dense than the sand. So you can get stuck, but you won't drown.

* * *

The "quick" in "quicksand" comes from the Middle English word that means "living," because the sand gives the impression of being alive.

Take It Slow

*T*rying to yank someone out of quicksand never works: You'd have to tug with the same force required to lift a mid-size car. If you are trapped in quicksand, small, subtle movements will liquefy the sand around your body, making it easier to extract yourself.

Built for Speed

*T*he British Automobile Association, or AA, was founded in 1905 as an organization dedicated to helping its members avoid police speed traps. Today it advocates for road safety and provides members with services such as driving directions, roadside assistance, and vehicle insurance.

Red Means Stop

*I*n the United States, someone runs a red light at an intersection once every twenty minutes.

WEIRD BUT TRUE

The Fast and the Furious

*H*ow fast is fast? You've probably heard of a nanosecond, which is a billionth of a second. Well that's just the beginning. One second can be divided into:

- a trillion picoseconds
- a quadrillion femtoseconds
- a quintillion attoseconds

* * *

The fastest laser light pulses ever recorded measured eighty attoseconds—that's eighty quintillionths of a second.

WEIRD BUT TRUE

Cuts Like a Knife

"*L*aser" is an acronym created by one of the pioneers of laser technology, Gordon Gould. It stands for "Light Amplification by Stimulated Emission of Radiation." The predecessor of the laser was the maser (Microwave Amplification by Stimulated Emission of Radiation) developed by a team led by Columbia University physicists Charles Townes and Arthur Schawlow. The two camps filed patents for their laser technology processes within nine months of each other, sparking one of the fiercest patent wars in history. Ironically, neither side can take credit for building the first working laser—that goes to Theodore Maiman of Hughes Research Labs, who successfully tested the ruby laser in May 1960.

Zap!

*D*evelopment of laser technology was instigated by the U.S. military, which envisioned lasers as "death ray" weapons. That's one task for which lasers have never proved useful.

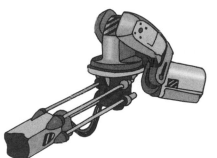

79

WEIRD BUT TRUE

It Was a Very Good Year

*I*n addition to lasers, a number of life enhancers were introduced in 1960:

- Etch A Sketch drawing toy
- Downy fabric softener
- Cardiopulmonary resuscitation (CPR) technique
- Bubble Wrap cushioning material

WEIRD BUT TRUE

Pops Like a Bubble

*M*arc Chavannes and Alfred Fielding created Bubble Wrap after experimenting unsuccessfully with an idea for plastic, textured wallpaper.

WEIRD BUT TRUE

Reason to Celebrate

$\mathcal{T}$he last Monday in January is officially designated Bubble Wrap Appreciation Day in the United States.

WEIRD BUT TRUE

Piece of Pi

$\mathcal{M}$arch 14 is Pi Day, so designated because the date—3-14—corresponds (at least in the way Americans write dates) to 3.14, the first three digits of pi, the mathematical ratio of a circle's circumference to its diameter.

* * *

The sequence of the digits in pi will not repeat, even if you calculate pi to the trillionth number past the decimal point. (It's been done!)

83

WEIRD BUT TRUE

Emerald Island

*T*he Caribbean island of Montserrat is the only place other than Ireland that celebrates St. Patrick's Day—March 17—as a national holiday. The first Irish Catholic settlers arrived on the island in 1632, ferried in from the island of St. Kitts, after the British Protestant governor ordered them to be driven out. Montserrat soon became a refuge for Irish Catholics, and by 1678 more than half the island's population had Irish roots.

WEIRD BUT TRUE

Fire Down Below

$\mathcal{M}$ ontserrat is a magnet for volcanologists (people who study volcanoes) from around the world. The island's Soufrière Hills volcano showed pre-eruptive seismic activity in 1992, and it's been erupting regularly ever since.

85

Hot Foot

*W*alking across hot coals hurts less than running across hot coals. Quick, light steps limit contact between the foot and the hot surface; running thrusts the foot against the ground more forcefully.

WEIRD BUT TRUE

On Your Toes

*W*alking on your toes requires 83 percent more energy than walking normally.

WEIRD BUT TRUE

This Little Piggy

*O*n average, 1.7 of every 1,000 babies
are born with polydactyly—the
presence of six or more toes on one foot,
or six or more fingers on one hand.

88

And *This* Little Piggy...

*O*ne of the oldest examples of a prosthetic appendage is an artificial big toe discovered on a female mummy found in Thebes in 2000. The toe is made from wood, carved and painted to look realistic, and attached to the woman's body with leather laces.

Finding artificial limbs on mummies and in tombs is not unusual—these nonfunctional prostheses were sometimes worn for purely cosmetic reasons or even attached after death so the body would appear whole in the afterlife. What makes this toe unusual is evidence of wear on the underside, indicating that the lady was walking around on it some three thousand years ago.

89

This Little Lizard

*I*f an axolotl salamander loses a leg, it will grow a new one in about three weeks.

Talkin' 'bout Regeneration

a powdered compound made from pig bladders could hold the key to regenerating human limbs. In a test case from 2005, a man who had accidentally severed off his fingertip was able to regrow it entirely in four weeks.

* * *

The U.S. Army is researching human limb regeneration because of its potential to help soldiers who have lost limbs in battle.

Plain as the Nose on Your Face

*a*fter losing his nose in a duel, the sixteenth-century Danish astronomer Tycho Brahe wore a prosthetic nose made from silver and copper for most of his life.

WEIRD BUT TRUE

Long Live the King (or Queen)

*D*enmark is Europe's oldest continuous monarchy; the current royal family can trace its roots back to the Viking king Gorm the Old, who ruled from around 900 to 940. Gorm's son and successor was Harald Bluetooth.

* * *

Bluetooth wireless technology was named for Harald Bluetooth, who united the nations of Denmark, Norway, and Sweden. The Bluetooth wireless logo is composed of the runes representing the letters H and B for "Harald Bluetooth."

93

Dynasty

$\mathcal{E}$mpress Maria Theresa of Austria earned the nickname "Mother-in-law of Europe." The only female ruler of the 636-year Habsburg dynasty, she ruled for 40 years and gave birth to 16 children. Those who lived to adulthood she married off strategically, pairing them with royals from other nations to strengthen the Habsburgs alliances. Her youngest daughter, and fifteenth child, would become Queen Marie Antoinette of France.

94

WEIRD BUT TRUE

Louis, Louis

*M*arie Antoinette's daughter Marie-Thérèse married her cousin Louis-Antoine, duke of Angoulême. He became King Louis XIX of France in 1830. His reign lasted twenty minutes.

* * *

The male heir to the throne of France is referred to as the dauphin. *Dauphin* is the French word for "dolphin."

Walk the Walk

*W*hen a wild dolphin became trapped in a marina lock in the 1980s, she was rescued and cared for at a dolphin sanctuary in Adelaide, Australia, where she must have picked up a few tricks from the other dolphins. Nearly twenty years later, marine biologists spotted several wild dolphins near Adelaide performing a trick known as tail walking—rising out of the water to a vertical position and gliding backward for several feet powered by flicks of the tail. Tail walking is a swell trick for trained performing dolphins, but it serves no known purpose in the wild. The biologists concluded that the rescued dolphin learned the skill during her time in the sanctuary and taught it to her pod-mates when she was returned to the wild.

96

WEIRD BUT TRUE

Sleep the Sleep

*D*olphins are "conscious breathers," meaning that they have to be awake, or semi-awake, to remember to breathe. If they fall asleep entirely, they'll stop breathing and drown. So, dolphins don't ever go completely to sleep. Instead, they rest in short bursts throughout the day, sometimes shutting one eye and resting half their brain while keeping the other eye open and the other half of the brain alert.

97

Naptime

*K*oalas sleep as many as twenty-two hours a day.

* * *

Koalas feed almost exclusively on eucalyptus leaves, which provide very little energy (thus the long naptime) and are highly toxic to almost all animals except koalas.

Don't Eat That!

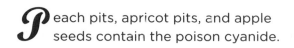

*P*each pits, apricot pits, and apple seeds contain the poison cyanide.

99

Take That

*a*ncient Hittites used diseased animals as weapons against their enemies the Arzawans during the Anatolian War in the fourteenth century BCE. Their species of choice were rabbits, sheep, and donkeys carrying the bacteria *Francisella tularensis*, which causes the infectious disease known as tularemia or "rabbit fever." Symptoms include skin ulcers, swollen lymph glands, fever, chills, respiratory failure, and pneumonia.

Whose Flus?

*I*n addition to avian (bird) flu and swine flu—both of which originated in animals and can affect humans—there are canine flu and equine flu, related diseases that affect dogs and horses respectively.

I Caught it from My Horse

*D*iseases that can be communicated from animals to humans are called zoonotic diseases. The most common of these is probably rabies, but there are others. People who work with horses may contract intestinal ailments, such as salmonellosis, and skin conditions, like ringworm and rain rot.

The Mosquito Nose

a mosquito's "nose" is located on its antennae, which are covered with what biologists call odorant receptors. The specialized receptors that are sensitive to human sweat are the ones that prompt a mosquito to bite. They're found only on female mosquitoes.

103

Last Bite

*I*t seems likely that King Tut died from malaria, a disease transmitted through the bite of a mosquito.

104

WEIRD BUT TRUE

You're Killin' Me!

*F*emale *Anopheles* mosquitoes, the ones that transmit malaria, are responsible for about one million human deaths each year.

Large and Lethal

*H*ippopotamuses are considered among the most lethal mammals on earth. They're very strong and aggressive, and they don't fear humans. Since they typically weigh between three and five tons, there's not much reason for them to be afraid.

Blood, Sweat, and Sunscreen

*W*hen hippos perspire, their sweat is red, which led to the belief that hippos sweat blood. Gross! And not true. Hippo sweat contains red and orange pigments, which make it look like blood, but these coloring agents act as a sunscreen to keep the hippo's virtually hairless skin from burning in the strong African sun. In addition, the red pigment seems to act as an antibiotic that helps wounds heal, which is quite handy since hippos tend to fight amongst themselves frequently and most wild hippos carry lots of battle scars.

Sensitive Skin

*P*igs, warthogs, elephants, and rhinoceroses can become sunburned. They roll in mud or sprinkle themselves with dust to protect their skin from the sun's UV rays.

Picture This

*H*ippopotamuses are depicted on the fifty-franc banknote from the African nation of Burundi and the two-emalangeni banknote from Swaziland.

* * *

Banknotes from Mozambique, Nepal, South Africa, and Tanzania all feature pictures of rhinoceroses.

WEIRD BUT TRUE

High Fives

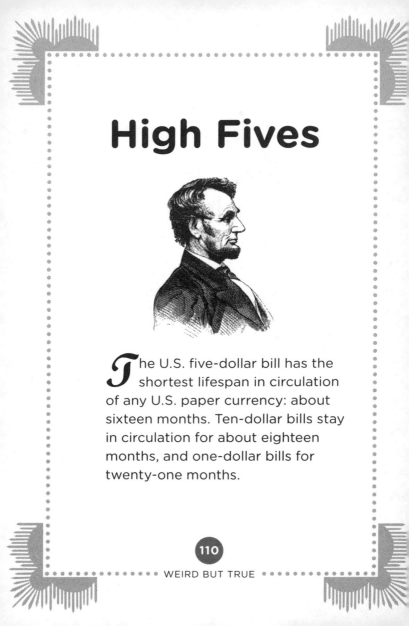

*T*he U.S. five-dollar bill has the shortest lifespan in circulation of any U.S. paper currency: about sixteen months. Ten-dollar bills stay in circulation for about eighteen months, and one-dollar bills for twenty-one months.

Loose Change

𝓘n 2009 the U.S. Mint produced 3.548 billion circulating coins; 2.354 billion of those were pennies.

* * *

Pennies contain more zinc than copper. Nickels contain more copper than nickel.

What the L?

$\mathcal{T}$he general manager of the mint in Chile was fired in February 2010 when it was discovered that thousands of fifty-peso coins had been issued with the name of the country spelled incorrectly: C-H-I-I-E instead of C-H-I-L-E.

Interestingly, the coins had been put into circulation in 2008; it took two years for the error to be reported.

112

WEIRD BUT TRUE

Three Rs
in Andorra

*T*he tiny principality of Andorra, located in the Pyrenees Mountains between France and Spain, has a literacy rate of 100 percent according to the *CIA World Factbook*. The entire country encompasses a little more than 180 square miles. Fewer than eighty-five thousand people live there.

113

Poetic Idol

*T*he most popular reality-television show in the Arab world is *Million's Poet*, a competition in which participants read their own poems in front of three judges, a live studio audience, and tens of millions of television viewers who watch the contest—broadcast live from Abu Dhabi—and vote for their favorite poets online and by text message. The winner receives a cash prize of 5 million dirhams, about $1.4 million.

It Could Be Verse

*T*he longest poem in the world is still being written, and it's growing by about four thousand verses a day.

A computer program created by Romanian web developer Andrei Gheorghe takes random tweets from the Twitter social networking service and pairs them into rhyming couplets that are then added to the collective work he calls "The Longest Poem in the World."

115

WEIRD BUT TRUE

And the Tweet Goes On...

*T*he *Mahabharata*, at some seventy-five thousand verses and nearly two million words, is one of the longest epic poems ever written and arguably the most significant Hindu text in history. Numerous translations and interpretations have been published, but one started in the summer of 2009 is among the more unusual: An Indian academic is writing his own interpretation of the *Mahabharata* on Twitter. Because of the service's message length restrictions, it is being published 140 characters at a time.

116

A Long, Long Time

*T*he eleventh-century Tibetan *Epic of King Gesar* is considered to be the longest epic poem in existence. It contains more than a million verses, most of which were not written on paper, but were passed down through generations by storytellers.

WEIRD BUT TRUE

Tell It Like It Is

*I*ndonesian novelist Pramoedya Ananta Toer composed his most famous work, the four-volume "Buru Quartet," during the ten years he was a political prisoner on Buru Island. Because he was forbidden to have pens or paper during most of his time in prison, he committed his stories to memory by telling them to his fellow prisoners every evening.

Inner Vision

*P*oet John Milton went blind, probably from glaucoma, in 1652. He wrote his masterpiece, the twelve-volume poem *Paradise Lost*, published in 1668, by dictating it to his daughters and assistants.

119

Sight to See

*W*e sometimes say that certain animals, such as rabbits, are "born blind." That's not entirely accurate. Rabbits are born with the ability to see, but their eyelids are temporarily sealed shut—a baby rabbit typically opens its eyes a week after birth.

WEIRD BUT TRUE

Multiplying Like Rabbits

*I*n the wild, a female cottontail rabbit may give birth to as many as six litters of four or more babies in one mating season. That's thirty-plus babies for one female in one season, which might be all she gets: Typical life expectancy for a rabbit in the wild is about one year.

WEIRD BUT TRUE

Who's Your Mama?

*I*n the original 1962 film version of *The Manchurian Candidate*, Angela Lansbury played Laurence Harvey's mother. She was not quite three years older than he was.

* * *

In the 1963 film version of *Bye Bye Birdie*, Maureen Stapleton played Dick Van Dyke's mother. She was six months older than he was.

WEIRD BUT TRUE

Who's Your Daddy?

*a*fter mating, the male midwife toad collects the female's eggs, wraps them around his hind legs, and carries them around with him for a month or more before depositing them in shallow water where they hatch into tadpoles.

Fear the Frog

Beelzebufo ampinga, the "devil frog," could be the largest frog that ever existed. It measured sixteen inches long and weighed about ten pounds; its mouth was enormous, and it was a predator. Fortunately, it became extinct about 65 million years ago.

Itty-Bitty Critters

$\mathcal{T}$he smallest snake known to science is *Leptotyphlops carlae*, the Barbados *threadsnake*, native to the Caribbean island of Barbados. A full-grown snake measures just four inches long.

* * *

The world's smallest seahorse is Satomi's pygmy seahorse, which measures only about half an inch.

125

Between the Shells

*P*earl oysters, the saltwater mollusks that produce pearls, are not closely related to the oysters we eat. So if someone tells you he found a pearl inside an oyster he was eating, it's probably not true. But. . .

Oysters aren't the only creatures that produce pearls. Other mollusks, such as mussels and clams, produce them too—and people have been known to discover pearls inside clams during a meal. Clam pearls are generally not as lustrous or as valuable as natural pearls found in oysters, although they can be quite beautiful.

126

WEIRD BUT TRUE

Wisdom of Pearls

*T*he largest pearl ever found was discovered in the Philippines, and it almost certainly came from a giant clam—the only creature big enough to have produced it. Known as the Pearl of Lao-Tzu or the Pearl of Allah, it measures nine inches long and weighs nearly fourteen pounds. It has been valued at between $40 and $60 million.

WEIRD BUT TRUE

Hot Ice

*a*t a high enough temperature, a diamond will burn.

WEIRD BUT TRUE

The Pain of Price

*P*aying too much for something activates the part of the brain that also is responsible for the perception of pain and guilt.

129

Hanging Empty

*I*n the early morning of March 18, 1990, two men dressed in police uniforms broke into the Isabella Stewart Gardner Museum in Boston, stealing thirteen works of art, including paintings and drawings by Vermeer, Rembrandt, Degas, and Manet. It was the largest art theft in history. More than twenty years later, the works have not been recovered and are valued today at around $500 million. In the museum, the frames of the stolen artwork remain in their places on the gallery walls as placeholders, empty and waiting for the return of the treasures.

* * *

According to the Art Loss Register, Pablo Picasso is the artist whose work is stolen most frequently. Hundreds of Picassos have been stolen from museums, galleries, businesses, and private homes, including a theft in 2007 from the home of Picasso's granddaughter.

130

WEIRD BUT TRUE

Artistic Irony

*I*n 1990 Vincent van Gogh's *Portrait of Doctor Gachet* set an all-time record for the highest auction price paid for a painting when it sold for $82.5 million at Christie's in New York. The van Gogh painting held that record for fourteen years, until Pablo Picasso's *Boy with a Pipe* sold at auction for $104.1 million in 2004.

* * *

Although scholars continue to hunt for documentation to the contrary, van Gogh appears to have sold only one painting during his lifetime. That was a piece called *Red Vineyard*, which sold in 1890 during an exhibition in Brussels.

131

The Disappearing Doctor

*V*an Gogh's *Portrait of Doctor Gachet* was bought at auction by Ryoei Saito, the head of a Japanese paper manufacturing company. Two days later, he paid more than $78 million for a painting by Renoir. Then he hid them both away in a warehouse—and declared that he loved the paintings so much he wanted them cremated along with him upon his death.

He later said he'd been kidding about the last part, but some people aren't so sure.

Saito soon ran into serious money troubles, followed by a conviction for trying to bribe a government official. He died in 1996.

And the paintings? Well, the Renoir was sold to help pay off Saito's debts. The van Gogh has vanished. Museum curators hope that the painting will surface again—and pray it didn't go up in smoke!

132

WEIRD BUT TRUE

On the Dot

*I*nstead of painting in long brushstrokes, French painter Georges Seurat painted with tiny dots of color, applying them one by one over an entire canvas. His most famous work is *A Sunday on La Grande Jatte*. It measures nearly seven feet high and more than ten feet across. From a few feet away, it's easy to distinguish the Sunday afternoon scene of people relaxing by the waterside, but up close the painting looks merely like random dots of paint—about 3.5 million dots of paint by some estimates.

* * *

It took Seurat about two years to complete *A Sunday on La Grande Jatte*.

133

The Art of War

*M*odern military camouflage was developed in France during World War I, initially to disguise vehicles—even battleships. The people who designed and executed the painting were fine artists in civilian life, and the seemingly random patterns of color blocks that comprised camouflage patterns were strongly influenced by the cubist paintings of artists such as Picasso.

* * *

American artist Grant Wood worked as a camouflage artist—a "camoufleur"—during World War I. Wood's most famous painting is the decidedly un-cubist, starkly realistic American Gothic.

134

Peace in Our Time

The Central American nation of Costa Rica has not had a standing army or navy since 1948.

Oscar Arias Sánchez, president of Costa Rica from 1986 to 1990 and again from 2006 to 2010, won the Nobel Peace Prize in 1987 for his work to draft the Esquipulas peace accords that helped prevent or end wars in El Salvador, Guatemala, Honduras, Nicaragua, and Panama.

WEIRD BUT TRUE

Error of Omission

*A*lthough he was nominated five times, the world's most famous pacifist, Mohandas K. Gandhi, never won the Nobel Peace Prize.

Colors of India

*I*n the center of the current flag of India is a twenty-four-spoke wheel that symbolizes forward progress. Originally, the wheel was a spinning wheel in honor of Gandhi's campaign to encourage people to make their own hand-spun, handwoven khadi fabric for their clothing. He viewed khadi as a symbol of self-sufficiency and unity for the Indian people.

* * *

The flag code of India states that all official flags must be made from hand-spun, handwoven fabric.

137

WEIRD BUT TRUE

Seeing Red
(and White and Blue)

*R*ed is the color seen most often on national flags. About 75 percent of the world's flags have red on them; about 70 percent have white.

* * *

At least twenty nations have flags of red, white, and blue (and only red, white, and blue). Among them: Australia, Cambodia, Chile, Cuba, France, Iceland, Laos, The Netherlands, North Korea, Norway, Panama, Russia, Taiwan, and the United Kingdom.

There's a Word for This, Too

*T*he study of flags is called "vexillology." This word comes from the Latin for "curtain."

What's Behind That Curtain?

*T*heater curtains that conceal the stage from the audience before the start of a performance, between acts, or at the end of a performance are a relatively new invention in theater terms. They didn't come along until after 1660. The ancient Greeks, who virtually invented theater, didn't have them. Neither did Shakespeare—his plays were usually performed in open-air venues where the stage was slightly sheltered but the audience was exposed to the sun and the rain.

Introducing Romeo and Juliet

*a*lthough he didn't have a theater curtain, Shakespeare did have the Curtain Theatre. Built in 1577 in an area known as Curtain Close, the Curtain Theatre is considered to be the second purpose-built theater in the London area. (The first was imaginatively named The Theatre.) It's likely that Shakespeare's *Romeo and Juliet* and *Henry V* had their debuts at the Curtain Theatre in the 1590s.

WEIRD BUT TRUE

No Girls Allowed

*D*uring Shakespeare's lifetime, boys or young men played all of the female roles in his plays—even romantic roles like Juliet. Most theatrical companies had only two or three boys in the troupe, which is why some scholars believe Shakespeare's plays have a lot more male roles than female roles in them.

* * *

The first woman to play a Shakespearean role on the public stage in England was Margaret Hughes, who played Desdemona in a 1660 performance of *Othello*.

WEIRD BUT TRUE

Vive la Difference

*T*heaters in France and Italy permitted women to work as stage actresses and performers in the sixteenth and seventeenth centuries, and those theatrical troupes performed in England as well. So English audiences did see women onstage—just not English women, who were banned by law from acting on the public stage.

WEIRD BUT TRUE

It's Curtains for You!

a hand-painted curtain that conceals the stage or that serves as a backdrop during a performance is not unusual—unless that curtain is painted by Pablo Picasso.

Sergei Diaghilev, founder of the Ballets Russes, managed to have some of the most renowned and unconventional artists of the early twentieth century design for his productions: among them, Henri Matisse, Juan Gris, and Joan Miró, as well as Picasso. They designed stage curtains, backdrops, and even costumes.

Matisse worked with Diaghilev only once— they didn't get along—but Picasso designed for at least six Ballets Russes productions. The first was the 1917 circus-themed ballet *Parade*, during which he met and married Olga Khokhlova, one of the ballerinas in the company.

144

Just Dessert

*P*erhaps the most famous ballerina to emerge from Diaghilev's Ballets Russes was Anna Pavlova. In the 1920s, Pavlova epitomized the ideal ballerina—light and ethereal, just like a swan—and just like the dessert named in her honor.

The Pavlova is made up of a meringue shell filled with tart, soft fruit, especially passion fruit, and sometimes topped with whipped cream. It's a simple dish with a complicated pedigree.

Anna Pavlova toured Australia and New Zealand in 1926. Her visit was such a great event that chefs in both countries claimed to have created the frothy, white dish inspired by her performance of the dying swan from the ballet *Swan Lake*. To keep both sides happy, it's often conceded that the dessert was developed in New Zealand, but was ultimately named in Australia. Still, that answer hasn't really settled the debate, which continues between the friendly rival nations to this day.

145

WEIRD BUT TRUE

New Word Order

*W*inston Churchill is credited with the first use of the phrase "Iron Curtain" to describe the emerging division in Europe between countries that were strongly influenced by the Soviet Union and those that were not. He used it in a speech he gave at Westminster College in Fulton, Missouri, on March 5, 1946.

Top Cats

$\mathcal{C}$hurchill owned a cat named Mr. Cat.

* * *

He also owned an orange cat named Jock, given to him by his private secretary Sir John "Jock" Colville. Churchill's former home at Chartwell—now a historic site—always has an orange cat named Jock living there.

147

Maybe "Mr. Cat" Isn't Such a Bad Name

*E*nglish author Thomas Hardy owned a cat named Kiddleywinkempoops.

148

Aren't You Glad You Know…

*C*at urine, like dog urine and human urine, contains phosphorous, which causes it to glow greenish yellow when it's exposed to ultraviolet light.

149

Starts With P

*T*he average person produces more than 10,000 gallons of urine and flushes the toilet 140,000 times in a lifetime.

Ends With U

*S*crabble players know that there are seventeen three-letter words that end with u on the Official Word List (OWL2) approved by the National Scrabble Association for tournament play in the United States. Among them is "ulu"—a type of knife used by Eskimo women to clean and skin fish, and the only three-letter word on the list that contains two *u*'s.

Two's Company

*a*s of 2006 when the revised Official Word List was issued, there are 101 two-letter words accepted in Scrabble tournament play in the United States. They range from "aa"—a type of lava—to "za"—a nickname for pizza.

Oh, K

*T*he chemical symbol for the element potassium is K. It comes from the Latin word *kalium*, which comes from *qali*, the Arabic word meaning "ashes."

* * *

It might seem logical that the chemical symbol for potassium would be P, but by the time potassium was discovered in 1807, there already was a P in the periodic table. P stands for phosphorus, which was discovered in 1669.

153

Okay, Kr

𝒯hese chemists who isolate new chemical elements just don't think ahead! By the time krypton was discovered in 1898 by Scottish chemist Sir William Ramsay and English chemist Morris M. Travers, "K" was already spoken for by potassium on the periodic table. So, the chemical symbol for krypton is Kr.

* * *

The name krypton comes from the Greek word *kryptos*, which means "hidden."

154

Greetings from Krypton

*a*round the time that the world was marking the fortieth anniversary of the discovery of krypton, the world's greatest superhero was about to make his comic book debut. The first appearance of Superman was in *Action Comics #1*, which was released in June 1938.

Superman, so the story goes, came to Earth from the planet Krypton. It's not clear why Superman creators Jerry Siegel and Joe Shuster chose to name the Man of Steel's home planet after an odorless, colorless gas.

155

Pocketful of Kryptonite

*I*n Superman comics, one of the few things that can defeat our hero is a strange metal called kryptonite that comes from the planet Krypton. Although the gas krypton exists, kryptonite does not.

WEIRD BUT TRUE

Not Okay

*J*erry Siegel and Joe Shuster, who created, wrote, and drew the original Superman, sold their rights to the character to DC Comics for $130 in 1938. Several years later, after the company had reaped millions from the Superman franchise, Siegel and Shuster tried to claim a share of the profits. Instead they were fired.

It took until 2009 for the Siegel and Shuster families to win a court case allowing them to reclaim their rights to Superman.

Oh, K2

K2, the second-highest mountain on Earth after Mount Everest, was named by Thomas Montgomerie in a geological survey he did in 1856. He called it K2 because it was the second peak he charted in the Karakoram mountain range of Pakistan, India, and China. ("K" for "Karakoram"; "2" representing the second peak.) When it was discovered that the local people had no particular name for the enormous yet remote mountain, the name K2 stuck.

WEIRD BUT TRUE

Be Careful Up There

*A*lthough K2 is not as high as Mount Everest, it's more treacherous. As of June 2008, Everest had 3,684 ascents and 210 fatalities in its history. K2 had 284 ascents and 66 fatalities.

* * *

Annapurna I is the most dangerous of the mountains known as "8000ers" (so named because they're higher than 8,000 meters [26,246.72 feet]). As of June 2008, 153 people had tried an ascent and 58 had perished in the attempt. Annapurna I, which is located in Nepal, is the tenth-highest mountain on Earth.

159

A New Level of Clean

*T*he Felsenputzer is a group of volunteer mountaineers who clean bird droppings from the mountainsides in Switzerland.

Point of View

Some mountain climbers set a goal of climbing the highest peaks on each continent. These peaks are referred to as the Seven Summits, although there are eight if you count both Carstensz Pyramid in Papua New Guinea and Mount Kosciuszko in Australia.

* * *

Erik Weihenmayer, who lost his eyesight at the age of thirteen, is the only blind person to have climbed all eight of the Seven Summits.

161

Ups and Downs

*M*ost great mountain ranges were formed by the shifting of tectonic plates beneath the Earth's surface. These shifts can also cause earthquakes. Figuring that what goes up eventually comes down, some geologists believe that tectonic shifts are now causing the Apennines mountain chain in Italy to collapse.

162

Recalculating Route

𝒯hanks to Global Positioning System (GPS) technology, geophysicists were able to determine that the entire city of Concepción, Chile, moved ten feet west in the February 2010 earthquake there. The same quake shifted Buenos Aires, Argentina—which is about 822 miles from Concepción—one inch to the west. And. . .

WEIRD BUT TRUE

In Space and Time

$\mathcal{T}$hat 8.8 magnitude earthquake shifted our planet on its axis by three inches, and shortened our days by about 1.26 milliseconds.

WEIRD BUT TRUE

The Space Between Us

The moon is moving away from Earth at a rate of about 1.5 inches each year.

WEIRD BUT TRUE

Can You Hear Me Now?

*E*ven though radio waves travel at the speed of light, a cell phone call from Earth to Mars would have a four- to twenty-minute time delay depending on how far the planets are from each other in their orbits at the time. A call from Earth to Jupiter would have a thirty-five- to fifty-two-minute delay.

What Did You Say?

*O*n Earth, there are an estimated 6,909 living languages, meaning ones used as the primary language of conversation in a community and taught to babies when they're learning to speak. (Sorry *Star Trek* fans: Klingon doesn't count.)

167

WEIRD BUT TRUE

I Can't Understand You

*M*ore than 450 languages have been designated as endangered; in other words, the number of people who speak these languages is dwindling and when those populations die out, there won't be anyone left who uses them. More than 70 endangered languages are (or were) native languages of the United States.

WEIRD BUT TRUE

We Don't Use That Sort of Language

*B*etween 2005 and 2009 it's estimated that ninety-one languages went "extinct," meaning that there are no longer any living native speakers. With the death of Chief Marie Smith Jones in 2008 came the death of Eyak, the language of the Eyak people of central Alaska.

* * *

The Bo or Aka-Bo language of India's Andaman Islands was classified as extinct in 2010 when the last native speaker died. Aka-Bo had been in use for more than sixty-five thousand years.

169

WEIRD BUT TRUE

It's Official

*W*ith eleven official languages, South Africa has the most official languages of any nation in the world. They are: Afrikaans, English, Ndebele, Sepedi, Southern Sotho, Swati, Tsonga, Tswana, Venda, Xhosa, and Zulu.

* * *

India has twenty-two commonly used languages, many of which are official languages in their particular states or regions; however, Hindi and English are the only designated official languages of India's national government.

You Can Say That Again

*M*andarin Chinese is the most widely spoken language on Earth. Spanish is second, followed by English, Arabic in all its forms, and Hindi.

171

Sing It Loud... Or Not

The national anthem of the Republic of Kosovo has no lyrics. It was chosen so that no preference would be given to one language over another. Kosovo, which declared its independence in 2008, has several commonly used languages, including Albanian, Serbian, Turkish, Roma, and Bosniak.

Words Can't Express

The national anthem of Spain, "La Marcha Real," also has no official lyrics, though there have been several attempts to introduce them, even as recently as 2008.

173

I Hear That

*a*n earworm is a repetitive, catchy song or piece of music that lodges itself in your brain and won't leave. Strategies such as listening to a different song or playing the earworm song in an effort to get it out of your head generally don't work, and might even make the situation worse.

* * *

Earworms almost always are songs or jingles with lyrics.

174

This Is So Disgusting We Can't Even Believe We're Writing It

Guinea worms enter the human body via drinking water. They're swallowed as tiny larvae that begin to grow almost immediately, burrowing through the intestines and winding through the body until they measure more than three feet in length. The human host is almost always unaware that the worms are growing until the creatures burst through the skin. The only way to remove a guinea worm is to pull it out, but this must be done slowly and carefully, and it can take months to remove the worm completely.

175

WEIRD BUT TRUE

Now the Good News

*P*rograms to ensure clean drinking water for communities have nearly wiped out guinea worm infestations in most of Asia and Africa. In 1986, when these programs began, there were an estimated 3.5 million cases of guinea worm disease in twenty countries; by 2009 that number was down to 3,500 cases in four countries. The aim is to eliminate guinea worm infestations entirely—and who could argue with that?

Write On

*D*ifferent systems of writing, such as Egyptian hieroglyphics and Babylonian cuneiform, were wiped out over time, even when the society's spoken language survived. One exception is the use of Chinese characters, which has continued for about three thousand years.

WEIRD BUT TRUE

Closed Captions

*a*rchaeologists at the Maya site at Calakmul, Mexico, unearthed large painted murals with hieroglyphic captions describing the action in the artwork—most of which related to food.

* * *

The Maya people of Central America had one of the first systems of writing in the New World. Evidence indicates that it could date back as far as 300 BCE. Archaeologists refer to the writing as hieroglyphs, even though the characters are unrelated to Egyptian hieroglyphics.

Prehistoric Primping

*a*t a cave in Spain, archaeologists found shells that had been pierced to be strung as necklaces, as well as traces of pigments that they think were used as cosmetic body paints by Neanderthals fifty thousand years ago.

Covering Grays

*a*ncient Greeks and Romans created a substance to darken their hair and cover their grays by making a paste of slaked lime (essentially limestone mixed with water) and lead oxide.

* * *

The Greek playwright Aristophanes mentions hair dye in the fourth century BCE. The Roman author Pliny the Elder and the Roman poet Ovid mention it in texts from the first century CE.

WEIRD BUT TRUE

Pale by Comparison

*P*remature gray hair is often caused by genetics. Although it happens rarely, some children are born with gray hair.

Red Roots

*D*NA from Neanderthals found in Spain and Italy indicates that the gene for red hair dates back to prehistoric times.

Big Red

*T*oday, redheads make up about 2 percent of the world's population.

* * *

Scotland is considered to have the world's highest percentage of redheads. An estimated 11 to 13 percent of the Scottish population has red hair.

183

Redheads Rule

*T*he amount of anesthesia given to a patient before surgery depends on a number of factors. One of them is hair color. A study at the University of Louisville in Kentucky found that redheads require about 20 percent more anesthesia before surgery than blondes or brunettes.

184

Mama Said Knock You Out

*E*ven though the administering of general anesthesia prior to surgery is intended to make the patient completely unaware of the operation, about 1 in every 863 patients under general anesthesia has some awareness or recollection of the surgical procedure.

...And You Will Know Us by the Trail of Germs

*T*here is only one you; and your germs prove it. Each individual carries about 150 species of bacteria on his or her hands, and every person's combination of bacteria is unique. The germs aren't necessarily dangerous, but they are distinctive; and scientists can tell where your hands have been simply by the germ samples they find on your phone, your computer, or other hard surfaces in your environment.

186

Sticking Around

$\mathcal{G}$erms that cause colds can live on hard surfaces such as faucets, handles, doorknobs, telephones, and television remote controls for as long as two days.

187

Not Dead Yet

*J*ust when they thought they could wipe out certain types of harmful bacteria, medical researchers discovered some that simply refuse to die. These are known as "persisters" because they seem to resist all the antibiotic treatments that should kill them. Instead, persisters go into a dormant state—playing dead without actually dying—so that someday, under the right (or wrong!) conditions, they can come alive again.

WEIRD BUT TRUE

Do as I Say, Not as I Do

*N*inety-two percent of Americans say that they wash their hands after using public restrooms; observational research says that only 77 percent actually do.

189

And That's the Truth

a 2002 study at the University of Massachusetts found that 60 percent of people lied at least three times in a ten-minute casual conversation.

* * *

The same study found that while men and women lie with about the same frequency, men lie to make themselves look better, appear more likable, or seem more competent, while women lie to make others feel better.

Department of Hair-Splitting

*T*he college professor who wrote the definition of lying for the *Stanford Encyclopedia of Philosophy* contends that an untrue statement isn't a lie unless the person telling it knows that it's false and says it anyway, with the intention to deceive another person.

So, if you believe something, it's not a lie.

Your Lying Smile

*H*ow can you tell whether someone who is smiling really means it? The answer lies in the eyes. The genuine human smile—the one that comes uncontrolled when you're truly happy or amused—is known as the Duchenne smile. It's named for a nineteenth-century French neurologist who determined that a fake smile is one that uses only the muscles surrounding the mouth, but a genuine smile engages the muscles around the eyes forming "crow's feet"—which ordinarily doesn't make people happy, but in this case perhaps we'll make an exception.

* * *

There is some evidence that people who smile genuinely most often tend to live longer.

WEIRD BUT TRUE

A Lie of the Mind

When you lie, your brain increases blood flow to the prefrontal cortex, the part of the brain that you use for making decisions, concocting stories, and distinguishing between right and wrong—the things you have to think about. When you tell the truth, your response tends to be automatic. You can answer without thinking, so the brain does not exhibit the same type of blood flow response.

193

WEIRD BUT TRUE

Brain Drain

*O*ver the past several thousand years human brains have gotten smaller. Anthropologists recreated the brain that would have fit inside a Cro-Magnon skull discovered in France. That 28,000-year-old brain would have been nearly 20 percent larger than today's human brain.

194

Remembrance of Places Passed

*I*f you have a great sense of direction, thank the neurons in your brain. Neurons known as "path cells" help you remember the direction you were traveling when you spotted a particular landmark. A separate set of neurons, known as "place cells," help you remember a place you've been. Together they work to get you where you want to go.

195

WEIRD BUT TRUE

This Looks Familiar

*M*agellanic penguins migrate by swimming from their homes in southern Chile and Argentina hundreds of miles north to the coast of Brazil each winter. They return to their birthplace for the mating season every spring.

WEIRD BUT TRUE

Haven't We Been Here Before?

*S*tudies have found that at least 60 percent of people (probably more) have experienced a sense of déjà vu. Episodes of déjà vu tend to decrease as you age.

* * *

Déjà vu does not require visual cues: Blind people experience déjà vu as often as sighted people.

197

WEIRD BUT TRUE

Repeat That

*K*arl Marx is often credited with coining the phrase "History repeats itself." However, he didn't actually write those words, and he never claimed them as his own.

The general idea came from a treatise written by the German philosopher Georg Wilhelm Friedrich Hegel. The politcal philosopher Friedrich Engels, Marx's friend and colleague, paraphrased Hegel's idea in a letter he wrote to Marx, and Marx later paraphrased it again in a pamphlet he wrote about French politics.

Never Seen That Before

*N*o two bolts of lightning are identical.

WEIRD BUT TRUE

Been There, Done That

*C*entral Africa experiences more lightning strikes than anyplace else on the planet. Lightning almost never strikes in the Arctic or Antarctica.

* * *

With hundreds of millions of lightning strikes on the planet every year—twenty million in the continental United States alone—there's no reason for scientists to believe that lightning can't strike the same place twice. In fact, they're pretty certain that it does.

200